Günter von Hummel

The Physically Sick Soul

Analytic Psychocatharsis as a new
Method for Psychosomatic and
Self-exercise.

The picture on the book cover depicts a Tranguloid which illustrates a mathematical calculation and incorporates a geometrical form meandering through topological surface. One could imagine the human body and soul to be just as intertwined and knotted up as in the illustration, hence so complex and difficult to recognize. Just so are the diverse psychological methods as in psychoanalysis on the one hand and different systems of meditative relaxation on the other. There are diverse, multifaceted scientific methods in dealing with this complexity and requires an experienced handling of structures, to open up and finally to reshape and mould it into a new form. I have named this procedure as '*Analytic Psychocatharsis*" because this method contains the form which entwines its way and connects the psychoanalytic insight of analysis with the purifying experience of catharsis (cleansing, meditative)

3. Edition 2021
Production and Publisher: BoD - Books on Demand, Norderstedt
ISBN 9783753473017
Translated from German by Paramita Müller-Lahiri

Table of Contents

1. Introduction

In this brochure I propose to illustrate a clear and simple concept of a psychotherapeutic method which satisfies the demands of modern scientific claims in its decisive precision (namely: *Analytic Psychocatharsis*). Perhaps this has a remote connection to I. H. Schulz`s method of 'autogenic training" especially in the so called 'advanced level'. In a similar way this method can be learnt and practiced at home if one studies the prospect carefully. Of course there is also the possibility of personal initiation. Nonetheless the reader should be prepared that the reading of the text is not so easy and completely unproblematic. This brochure does not deal with the usual treatises; which for example suggest positive thinking as a way of solution for depression resulting or as a consequence of false thought. This is not a booklet providing warm hearted advices and simple solutions. The method introduced in this prospect not only differentiates but also distances itself from even more demanding methods such as the so called 'alternative' psychotherapeutic practices.

There are innumerable methods as mentioned below but often have the disadvantage of offering easy solutions to complex problems. Methods like different forms of meditation as a form of relaxation or consultation in the form of conversation have also their limitation. Though apparently clear, simple and an easy way of resolving problems these diverse diversion therapies are not professional or rather not based on sufficient scientific knowledge.

Psychoanalysis is one of such methods that acquires the criteria expected of scientific methods namely, precision; even though the theoretical background and therapeutic procedure is very complex and complicated. Though psychoanalysis is a lengthy process of long duration and quite circumstantial it is nonetheless scientifically precise. My procedure in *Analytic Psychocatharsis* certainly achieves simplicity as well as clarity as in all authentic scientific methods through a starting point that one finds in several domains be it culture, 'spirituality" or different sciences. Much of it is based on psychoanalysis yet the essential element, the very foundation stands on its own right and is not so complex or complicated. (At a later stage certain theoretical aspects necessitates detailed explanation and may be of interest to some readers but for practicing this experience or method it is not essential for each individual to delve into this.) Hence the theoretical part of the text is entirely optional and is left to the user to decide for oneself. The intellectual approach is not necessary by satisfying a scientific ambition but for security and confidence in the method.

To reveal a clue in advance at what is to follow I want to point out that *Analytic Psychocatharsis* does not hide behind the facade of preconceived concepts or pre-given notions of meditative concentrative methods that shows the way or promises to find the true solution. Neither does this method adopt the classic form of 'free associations' practiced in psychoanalysis where the patient is compelled to re account spontaneous thought and ideas sometimes rather absurd, perhaps somewhat whimsical or even deeply embarrassing. This is due to the fact that the *unconscious* itself is embedded within the deep crevices of the mind/soul and contains or hides the profound truth leading to a solution. The *Analytic Psychocatharsis* works with formula-like word formulations, that carries several meanings (Formula-Words) and due to this it is purely formal, purely structural and contains within itself the solution; whose truth the practicing user must personally experience and deepen to gain both, namely Solution / transformation (catharsis) and Truth (analysis). All that is needed to achieve this is that the practicing user sits relaxed and reposed and in thought practices the formulations, and after that in the second exercise allows the answers to arise from the unconscious.

Briefly: *Analytic Psychocatharsis* responds to the elementary question concerning transformation involved with the quest of healing and to find the real answer. This is the aim and target of all therapeutic methods to find a truth that enhances a transformation and heals. The truth is very often hidden in the question placed. The answer is very often concealed in the question if not completely but at least partly and certainly. Hence every question contains the answer though not obvious at first glance or revealed in the surface at face value but nonetheless in an authentic scientific manner. Since the *unconscious* has its own dynamic and behavioral pattern (The request placed in the question itself is not fulfilled as it appears in the foreground and predominates in the form of a wish or request that is contained in the question. In other words the request is not granted because the question proposed is too ostensible, or too wish oriented)

But when I put a question or replace a request by a formula or word- formation my own *unconscious*, which has its own protective mechanism and often guards itself from outside intrusion, will be compelled to provide an answer. The *unconscious* working of the mind includes the essential truth arising from the depths of the soul. The answers are constituted, included within the realms of the *unconscious* work of truth. Or the request is returned in a contrapuntal form (since the *unconscious* has its own way of working, as Freud formulated it anticathexis) yet the request is fulfilled in a precise form. The purpose of this method presented here is to fulfill the request, to find the true sense of the inner meaning rising from the depths of the *unconscious*. The aim of this text is to find the real answer or the truth from the *unconscious* working of the mind in a precise scientific manner, a quest which is not unscientific.

The just mentioned basic elements consist of two basic principles. The two basic principles or drives are further developed and worked out in psychoanalysis and which according to J. Lacan works similarly in every human being. The pattern and the principle is the same:

(a) In an elementary drive of perception named / termed just by Freud as the *scopic-* or *looking drive* (scope /observation).

(b) A similar basic drive a drive of expression named by Lacan as the *speaking drive* (invocative drive).[1]

Basically the drives deal with that what Goethe has described so: 'Two souls alas! Are dwelling in my breast; and each is fain to leave its brother. The one, fast clinging, to the world adheres with clutching organs *(scopic drive)*, in love's sturdy lust; the other strongly lifts itself from dust to yonder high, ancestral spheres *(speaking drive)*." These drives (pulsations, powers) are conceptualized in psychoanalysis not as directly experienced or even practicably lived out. This becomes apparent to us when we are conscious of the form. When we are confronted and faced with the physical representation of the forms depicted in ideas, imagination, feelings, fantasies and symptoms. A certain problem begins to crop up here.

---

[1] At another point I have explained (the 'conjectural thinking", BOD 2004) that these two basic drives are also valid in physics and arts. The psychoanalyst speaks here about drives, instincts or urges.

As psychoanalytic methods point out man defends himself against too strong forces and difficult endeavours, which the controlling intensity of these drives seems to incorporate. In other words man tends to protect himself by creating emotional 'defense mechanism' against such power or drives in the form of concealing, clamming-up, restraints, obstructions and blockings. The aim of psychoanalysis is to unlock the 'defense mechanism' and reveal the hindrance or obstruction and finally to find a solution. Often a very long-winded process is needed to break down the resistance, to unlock the hidden door of the mind, consuming long hours of analysis, hence circumstantial in its method.

Also in *Analytic Psychocatharsis* these factors have to be considered: the connections between restraints, defense mechanism and the power- drives. But the procedure is entirely different in this method, it is reversed here. Here the power-drives will be directly experienced, be it psychical, yes even psychosomatic though the emphasis is not so much on the 'defenses' or blockings but rather on a formal direct manner, restricted and governed by the principle of form. The defense mechanism or restraints in this case i.e. *Analytic Psychocatharsis*, is avoided, circumvented and even leveled out. Nonetheless what is defended, resisted will be substantially comprehended, considered and worked out.

To represent this in simplified terms, the effect these basic elements have (power – drives) that I have just mentioned I would like to name the *scopic drive* as *Id Rays*. At this stage one is arriving to the point of clarity, namely a comprehending structure of power- drive which is experienced directly and immediately by every human being. All that is required is that one sits down quietly for a while, undisturbed from outer distractions, inert, concentrating in a relaxed manner with closed or half open eyes. The emphasis is on the effortlessness and concentration of the moment where the appearance of the phenomena *Rays*.

One is aware of it as e.g. as a sentiment of luminance, as an experience of alleviation, release, or even an inner perception of change in the body image. Which means that the self-perception of one`s image; the pictorial image of one-self, the body -image undergoes a change. One can be aware of this shortly before one falls off to sleep, or waking up briefly when the sensomotoric 'nerve currents' disappear or appear again. At the moment, perhaps even very briefly when the consciousness of body-image undergoes a change. This can appear in the form of shivering-through, or dissociating or by a feeling of a room enlarging. Manifestation can vary but what is significant is that this phenomena *Rays*.

In a similar manner I wish to shorten the expression- or *speaking drive* in a simplified term namely *Id Speaks*.

This also corresponds to the psychoanalytic opinion of the physical *unconscious* which I mentioned earlier. Namely not something that has a being but that which has something to s a y, something to utter and communicate. *Speaks* so to s a y, or utters. It is not so easy to understand this but I shall make an attempt to make it comprehensible so that the reader is able to understand this phenomena. Even better formulated would be an explanation that there is something within us that constantly whispers, mumbles, rustles and speaks often experienced in brief moments of awakening up. (e. g. even strange, confusing thoughts that mumble and whisper in half sleep, just before one wakes up really or even confused words that shake and jostle like a babble of nonsense making no sense. This is the point of alertness just before one wakes up from sleep)

2. Preliminary Practice

Not to get too caught up in the theory and complicate matters at this stage I would like to propose a preliminary practice in the *Analytic Psychocatharsis* which shall be elaborated later on. Above all I wish to emphasise the scientific aspect of *Analytic Psychocatharsis*. 'Radiat' in Latin is namely *Rays*. 'Dicit' is *Speaks*. As emphasised earlier on, *Rays* is an abbreviation of the earlier mentioned *scopic drive* based on the strength of vision; that what one perceives visual virtuality. *Speaks* is an abbreviation of the *speaking drive* based on the strength of

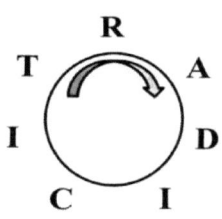

symbolic expressions. If we combine or rather merge both the Latin expressions to 'Radicit' we have a *Formula-Word* whose composition and main characteristic contains a clear and precise scientific method. There are several overlapping meanings written in this circulatory expression, as will be illustrated later on. The fact that the two terms (*Rays / Speaks*) occur in it is only a secondary effect. It is more important to see the nature of the overlapping meanings, depending on the letter from which the formula word is read.

To begin with it one sits down in a relaxed, comfortable manner with half opened or closed eyes and in thought

slowly repeats 'Radicit' in a monotone and simultaneously is aware of a characteristic that *Rays* one could even
begin to feel a sense of relaxation, or even a sense of
catharsis; a feeling of liberation, of unbinding and of
loosening. The slow, monotonous repetition of 'Radicit'
in mental spheres promotes the withdrawal inward and
thus the emergence of the *Rays* experience which has
nothing to do with the seeing eyes but rather an inner
vision, an inward perception, the *unconscious* body image representations. The, mirroring of perception drive
promotes or perhaps leads to a stage of inner retreat. Lacan is speaking here of phosphorescence.[2] The inner seeing that which *Rays* and the mental repetition of the *Formula-Word* 'Radicit' in thought is the initial exercise or
practice. This will be explained in greater detail later. At
this point a small experience may suffice since I deliber-
ately do not wish to manipulate suggestions as to what
one is.

If one sits in a calm reposed manner for a while and is
composed within there is a feeling or a sensation of slight
change in the body. It could deal with parts of the body
image or the phosphorescence – as just mentioned above.
For example arms and legs could be slightly 'numb'
heavy or light; around the trunk there could be a tingling
sensation, a kind of catharsis evoked in the feeling of a

---

[2] Lacan, J., Seminar V, Turia and Kant (2006) P.. 371

noticeable 'shivering, tingling flow" running through. This experience is recollected or felt at the moment just before one sleeps. No matter what happens or does not happen the repetition of the *Formula-Word* 'Radicit' simultaneously with the perception of *Rays* as I have named it in an abbreviated form results in a liberating feeling of relaxation. It is more than sufficient to experience a minimal feature of the above mentioned phenomena.

After a while (perhaps ten minutes) one can practice the exercise which I term as *Speaks*. This follows the first exercise which consist of the slow repetition of R-A-D-I-C-I-T practiced with short intervals or interruptions; an inner murmur at the background rotating in thought and perhaps the sensation or feeling of catharsis begins currently to occur. The concentration now is focused on sound a rustle or a murmur, a tone or tune and this necessitates a still, motionless tranquility, and a retreat from distracting noises of the outside world especially at the initial stage.[3] It now requires an introverted relaxed concentration; the tone emerges from the depths of one's being arising from the depth to the height which in this

---

[3] I refer concerning that tone or tune to the psychoanalytic conception of 'Sound-Object'. That means an inner psychic object which is constructed by the voice of the mother in early childhood. Lacan is speaking here from the 'universal murmur' as a whispering reporting in the unconscious which is used for concentration.

case towards the head (central or towards the right).[4] This `sound` tone or murmur is an intonation so to say as a *Speaks*. This experience *Speaks*: as though a thought is formulated arising from a distant horizon or it could even be a spontaneous fleeting unexpected 'sound' that *Speaks*. This 'slogan' can be a brief accumulation of phrases, a huddled murmur of words or `talk` that seems to appear from nowhere, a kind of strange idea arising from nonentity making itself felt, tangible and present as a consequence of the attention to the exercise that one has delved into. Certainly this is not a 'babble" of confused words but a clear thought process as a result of the thought process and concentrated repetition of the psycho-linguistic structured *Formula-Word*. Hence a logical sequence, a natural consequence and a result of the exercise that one has practiced. This is not an acoustic hallucination but rather an experience of the primal process of the drive to speak.

Towards the end of this exercise an individual method of 'Radicit' is then established, a connection between a *Rays* and a *Speaks*; a *Speaks* that *Rays* and vice versa. Interchangeable and intertwined a 'Radicit' so to say. Hence an experience of order is achieved in the relationship of the fundamental basic drives, a strength arising from the interpretation of connections. It is not expected that one

---

[4] That instruction deals with the brain-lefterity and so corresponding to the dexterity of speaking.

achieves perfect results at the very first attempt neither it is expected that one grasps and understands this method at an initial stage. All that is awaited or expected is that one accepts this method as the first step towards an *Analytic Psychocatharsis* and also a better understanding of the preliminary exercise that has been introduced so far; also from the aspect of an exercise. This is the initial step towards a better comprehension or even clarity of what *Analytic Psychocatharsis* is trying to represent.

Then hereupon – on practice - lies the focal point of the procedure especially for severe sick people. Certainly psychoanalysis offers also suchlike patients intensive aid. But analyst F. Henningsen writes that in a serious case (traumatization in early childhood) more than eight hundred therapeutic sessions are necessary (4 x a week for about 6 -8 years).[5] Most people could not pay such a therapy. Nevertheless psychoanalytic theory is important for *Analytic Psychocatharsis* because of its scientific security. (For a **simplified reading** the theoretical explanations beginning from here till to the **page 22** could be skipped).

Both 'Power-drives' mentioned earlier on exist in the classical structure of psychoanalysis. On the one hand the drive conceptualized by Freud is called the *scopic -drive*: perception-drive (and formulated by me as the drive of

---

[5] Henningsen, F., Psychoanalysis with Traumatisized Patients, Klett-Cotta (2012)

perception or sensory seeing) which I have not only adopted in the truest sense of its concrete meaning but have also directly represented it here as *Id Rays*. Neurologists talk about 'mirrored' cerebral activities.[6] In other words cerebral activities in the brain has an *unconscious* mirrored structure that reflects itself in the sense that all physical functions are 'mirrored' or as physicians claim that any illness will have a corresponding focus point in the brain, which collaborates with the illness.[7]

Almost any physical illness also contains an aspect that pertains to the nervous system, the psyche or the *unconscious*. Scientifically such a focus point has not been found and this is typical of 'brain research" to delve into hair-splitting debates and to find methods of measuring. This does not say much since who could find an interconnection between nerves and disease or in other words to measure nerve cells that corresponds to an illness. What is often ignored or rather neglected then is the true or significant target of reaching the correct meaning, the actual message or the authentic naming of rhetorical symbolism (*Speaks*). Especially when psychosomatic

---

[6] Neurologists speak of ‚mirror-neurons' i. e. nerve cells which handle mirroring processes and are combined in that mirroring function in the brain. That is corresponding psychological with the 'mirroring state' in early childhood which creates the first ego in form of selfreflecting imagines.

[7] Solms, M., Turnbull, O., The Brain and the Inner World, Patmos (2004)

disturbances emerges this method of measuring fails to find a solution and physicians are often at a loss to find the real symptoms.

Nevertheless one could think the following, simply formulated it consists of concurring 'mirrored" process or even better, *unconscious* mental reflection, that is to say a kind of *Rays* which can be experienced as cleansing, yes even as a direct inner tingling (as in body image) or as a sensation of luminosity or a feeling of joy or as catharsis.[8] On the other hand it is a matter of rhetorical 'wording" or word-representation a kind of *Speaks.* This contains in other words something like an inner monologue that one constantly experiences that can be seized, captured, felt and in this way 'relinquished'. In this context J. Lacan speaks of 'typographic space'[9] and of 'inner syntax' (monologue?) which is in every human being.[10] It is not something that incorporates a being but something which has something to say that also expresses itself in us constantly (something that continuously carries on in us as soliloquy (inner monologue).

---

[8] I like to give a quotation here from Goethes 'Faust' where the poet says: 'The shivering is the best share of humankind". That means the trickling or shivering through running down the back. Greek kathairo means cleaning and deals with the same experience.

[9] Lacan, J., Seminar V, Turia and Kant (2006) P. 176

[10] Lacan, J., The Psychoses, Quadriga (1981) P. 135

Naturally there are quite normal ways of regulating these power- drives and the resisting 'defenses" as mentioned earlier on, and we do this constantly. We do this in the form of what one calls sublimation. By sublimation one understands the improvement, uprating, mandating of these *unconscious* power-drives in the level of the conscious, in social spheres and general life. The uncontrolled power -drives can be steered and regulated in all aspects of existence: be it work, art, culture, physical activities, social contacts and many other spheres so that the conscious awareness of everyday living can be lived in a normal manner with its norms of 'normal' emotions and feelings. So some aspects of sublimation are more intellectual, others more related to body oriented activities or some expressed in emotions and feelings.

The picture (Pict: 1) below shows the different possibilities of sublimation illustrated on the Boy-Surface as background (connecting: body/ physical activities, emotions and feelings and the intellect/ intellectual occupation). The individual names are only designations or labels taken from different cultural spheres, psychotherapeutic methods or other options; subjective, decisive choices confronted by man as an integral entity. The personal choice faced by the subjective uniqueness of man as a complete individual. The Boy-Surface represented in the picture is like a loop somewhat like the cover of an envelope thus depicted as a mathematical theorem. This demonstrates in a new facet, the multiplicity contained within the nuances of a unified formulation. This is of central significance and importance in understanding *Analytic Psychocatharsis* (marked with the letters AP here).

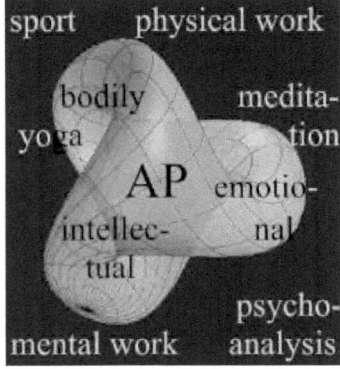

Psychoanalysis is a very intellectual method predominantly occupied with the realms of the mind (i.e. psychic) and spiritual (i.e. soul) and within the analytic process a great deal is revealed surfacing from psychic-soul. Despite its broad spectrum psychoanalysis has its limitations because it lacks the corporeal aspect since the emphasis is not body oriented. In today`s world this lack of physical or body-oriented practices is a decisive problem. For instance who would be willing to invest hours in psychoanalytic conversational therapy if he or she is suffering from migraine or stomach aches? The patient may find a bit of relief from his complaints, pains and suffering but not the release from the direct ailment even though this is closely connected and embedded in the seam of his body and soul.

Even so less in connection to this aspect can sport by itself help to solve psychosomatic illness since sport too has its limitation; while the connection between the inner spiritual power-drives are not resolved alone through physical activities. Just as analytic -therapy alone in its own standing cannot help to bring relief to psychosomatic illness since it ignores the physical aspect to a great extent. Even art, yoga and other psychotherapeutic methods to name a few, though quite effective in many ways is nonetheless not sufficient to cure or heal the 'physical sick soul'. As specified earlier on, even religion, family and intimate relationship are not enough factors to heal and cure since these too are limited. From the therapeutic stand point or domain all the above mentioned criterion or principles to have their limitation, and in addition does not feel the responsibility to do so. Despite all sublimations a residue of the *unconscious* rest remains in day to day life.

The remaining rest are the uncontrolled power-drives and the 'defense –mechanism' which can make the soul sick despite all forms of healthy conditions and good lifestyles; then the need for psychotherapy becomes necessary. One has often mentioned that this is good for all. Psychoanalysis has shown to us that in the therapy we transfer unconsciously the whole packet of uncontrolled power-drives and the 'defenses' as well to the analyst. The meaning (unresolved power -drives and 'defenses') is transferred which mostly originate from earlier conflicts or earlier relationship (therefore one calls this process the transference). With the help of an interpretation these transferences are shifted to a form called 'free-association" (expression of free ideas) based on what the patient reveals or conceals and with this information, which is the *unconscious* rest, the analyst can find the connections. Exactly this occurs in *Analytic Psychocatharsis*, the connections, that is the interpretation of meaning and transference but in a completely different manner. This will be elaborated later. At this juncture instead of being too entangled in theory and more theory a shift to the practical part of *Analytic Psychocatharsis* is called for. The practice anyway explains the theoretical aspect more clearly. I wish to only emphasise with this introductory remark that despite everything psychoanalysis in a simplified scientific manner is fundamentally important as a tool.

3. Aspects of Psychoanalysis

In the *Analytic Psychocatharsis* we sit in a comfortable position and 'bundle" our ideas and thoughts, quite unlike the method of 'free association' adopted in psychoanalysis to initiate the *transference.* Neither do we meditate on any kind of mythical / mystical method. We concentrate from the beginning repeating mentally the so called *Formula-Words.* With 'RADICIT" as one formulation staying on the border of language I have only attempted to introduce a preliminary exercise. The 'free associations' in psychoanalysis are also similar in the sense that they too are on the border of language because the expressions are often incoherent, spontaneous, and chaotic. The free ideas but note they are very much rooted in direct speech communicated through every day colloquial language. No one actually freely 'associates'. So interpretation of the 'free associations' is always difficult and needs a lot of time.

In *Analytic Psychocatharsis* such a procedure corresponding to psychoanalysis is rather given in the sense that it already exists not by *transference* that one shifts or transfers to a person sitting next to us (in case of psychoanalysis) to the analyst. But the person exercising *Analytic Psychocatharsis* has to transfer to a nonentity, to a void of nothingness, a free empty darkness that stretches and merges ahead of him. It is similar to meditation or 'autogenic training" since the starting point begins in a similar way; namely that one sits in a relaxed manner, dwells in nonentity and in thought repeats *the Formula-Words*, whereby spontaneity and associations are included mentally into this space of free nothingness. However this space is already a little bit pre-interpreted through the *Formula-Words* so that interpretation is not always necessary. So also in *Analytic Psychocatharsis* interpretations would remain difficult but at a later stage I shall explain how a satisfying interpretation does ultimately and finally emerge.

Id Rays and *Speaks*; within our *unconscious* the image - and the word representations are constantly interrelated and linked together. The more deficient and *unconscious* this link or connection is, the more are the psychosomatic ailments, the more are the traumas, disorders and other psychological afflictions (constraints, repressions, splits, inhibitions, defense mechanisms and blockings) to name a few. Of course other significant aspects play a major role in this interlinking or interrelationship for instance the inclusive influential factors or objects of the outer world, the connection with the surroundings, (which also includes human factors ' objects') as well. In the classic form of psychoanalysis the word representation could appear in the consciousness emerging from the *unconscious* in the form of dreams and dream interpretations, over the so called 'free associations' and their interpretation or over the empirical experience or interpretation of faulty achievements or slip of the tongue. Though the image representation is included, as mentioned, the implication is often insufficient since it is not close enough to physical vicinity. As observed, the classic or traditional form of psychoanalysis is too complex, complicated and far stretched as in the method adopted by a body -oriented psychotherapy.

Meditative methods have an advantage over other methods in that it contains the body- and image-oriented aspect as well, as experienced in the context of practice. Yet it also has its disadvantages too, in that too much of intentional knowledge or awareness is already given or even better explained - the thought and the meaning, the theme and the sense as base is already present. This method has a very resolute form; chosen, defined and preconceived by the teacher of meditation. This method is far more comprehensible than the method of psychoanalysis since it is more image representative, transparent, graphic and also demonstrative. (*Rays*) But what is often neglected ignored in this method and which is so essential for psychoanalysis is the emphasis on the *unconscious* that is the word-representations, the wordiness, the symbolic imprints of language (*Speaks*, invocative drive). This aspect cannot be undermined since it is a very significant and essential criterion of psychoanalysis, because this is what that makes it scientific and substitutes the dependence on therapists. Nonetheless we take the support of meditative methods since it is close to immediate practice.

All though both therapeutic methods appear to be contradictory at first glance they are not so disparate after all since psychoanalysis and meditative methods (e.g. autogenic training) apply clarifying tools to connect and distinguish certain fixed ideas and definitions to achieve the same, hence very similar: The analyst listens to the patient with an *evenly suspended attention* as Freud named it, just as the person practicing meditation is compelled to listen to the inner self within with the same suspended attention. In the same manner 'free associations' corresponds (the free ideas or associations in the analysis) to the apparent free and different meanings in the *Formula-Words* and appearance of some free ideas in meditation as I have just mentioned above. So unspecific thoughts are pushed aside but as much however bound or guided by simple instructions; for instance through *Formula-Words*, structures can be brought forward.[11]

The analyst during the process of psychoanalysis is certainly more personally present (as object of transference and as interpreter). Al though through the countertransference of the patient to the analyst and also through

---

[11] The word, 'guided" in meditation is not contradictory to thought process in meditation. Thoughts cannot be all together avoided. But a structured 'guidance" in the formal sense is an ideal way to resolve the problem.

the aspect of his reality it can be more of a hindrance or an obstruction.[12] In Meditation contrarily the physical presence of the teacher remains in the background. Transference occurs here in so called virtual space, in nothingness so to say. One has often termed this as wild transference or transference outside the framework of analysis. I term it also as primal –transference, which finally is nothing more than *Speaks* (e.g. also in the *Analytic Psychocatharsis*) which reveal or answers from the realm of apparent nothingness while in the classic or traditional form of psychoanalysis a long process and exchange of speech is necessary to work out a solution.

When the combined knots between the two basic drives tighten, narrow or tilts too much towards *Rays* then a repetition overshadows and dominates. The knots tighten even further and are far more fixed inside the *Rays*. Then the compulsion towards repetition within the *unconscious* is persistent so to say. Quite often the traditional form of psychoanalysis is unable to loosen or disperse the knots since the knotted combinations are too intertwined and fixed. As mentioned, the combination of conflicts, drive

---

[12] Counter-transference means the transference in the opposite direction as a reaction of the analyst to the transference of the patient. Problematical is also the 'evenly suspended attention' of the analyst. He could never go so deep into himself and at the same moment remain aware of the expressions and formulations of the patient. The attention in meditation is also deeper.

forces are then coerced into repetition; the complexity of the *Rays/ Speaks* connection is also revealed within. This repetition is of a completely different kind in *Analytic Psychocatharsis*. What occurs here, in *Analytic Psychocatharsis* as already suggested is that compulsive repetition is reversed; what was coercive repetition in classic forms of analysis now shifts to a repetition of linguistic Formula. That which was defined as sick and repressive compulsive repetition in analysis is now the central complex point of focus in *Analytic Psychocatharsis* – the repressive compulsions are gathered, captured or perhaps shifted to *Formula-Words*, suspended evenly and eventually, lastly integrated in the therapy. Through the forced repetition of psycho -linguistic structural help the *unconscious* is compelled to an interpretation and the drive for coercive repetition within the *unconscious* is canalized or even more appropriate is contrarily poled. Some writers name this form of repetition as 'good repetition".

Whilst in Psychoanalysis active repeated sequence is observed as disease and neurotic disorders; in *Analytic Psychocatharsis* contrarily the repetition is a part of the exercise, a conscious practice and process of learning_ 'learning- repetition" and not a disturbed, diseased, neurotic compulsive, repetition. One could assume that during the practice of alternative methods like Autogenic Training, Behavioral Therapy or diverse methods of Meditation which work as mentioned already too much determined the therapist is provided with a good access to the knotted *Rays/Speaks* disposition. One needs to repeat this exercise so long till the narrow fixations are annulled and cease to be of any importance. One senses that in these methods one is quite dependent on the outlook, concept and pre-notion of the therapist and hence one is indirectly influenced by the approach of the therapist or the teacher. Though *Analytic Psychocatharsis* contains certain features of these methods, (the aspect of meditation for instance), it is quite different in that the dependency is non-existent. It offers structural help, which is already present within the *unconscious* as a formula and in addition a regulated application of psycho- linguistic order. It presupposes that the unconscious knows everything at least substantially more as the conscious as Freud has always emphasised: 'The unconscious does not render a judgment or a calculation but it knows"!

4. Reapplication of Exercise

At this stage now, I suggest for a better understanding a renewal of the two practical exercises. The technique is uncomplicated even simple as I wish to emphasise; all one needs to do is to sit in a comfortable position and to repeat in thought at a slow pace the *Formula-Words*. Just to repeat one after another two or till five *Formula-Words*[13] and at the same time to pay attention to the emergence of what appears and has the characteristic of *Rays*. Initially during the second exercise (see later) through a kind of concentration one arrives at an answer (full *Speaks, Pass-Word*) to the first exercise. During the act of *Rays*, the act itself can be a light point, a gleam, a luster, a ray, an illumination or an elucidation, or a pictorial perception of a body in the form of a picture or a symbol. Lacan speaks about this as a kind of Phosphorescence as has been mentioned. In the same manner one can have a sensory experience, as a shivering, trickling through,[14] it can be just black points or a sea of black

---

[13] Further *Formula-Words* are available at the web-page situated on the last page of this booklet and are also published in other books.

[14] That deals with an experience of some atavistic feelings. The early man could communicate much more as we now by feeling and tasting with his bare and exposed skin. The shivering through can be experienced by listening to emotional music (audible means / sensation). In *Analytic Psychocatharsis* it is

visualized through closed eyes and it can also be a feeling, a perception that one's physical bodily existence is remote and somewhat far, perhaps widened, even detached or shivering. Since the color black is deep seated in our head, a part and parcel of darkness, an expression of night it is not that easy to ignore, eliminate or remove black. A residue remains. It does not really matter in which form, color or the way one has experienced, seen and felt this, what counts is the fact that it has the characteristic of *Rays* even if it is somewhat reduced. It suffices to have sensed this *Rays*.

It is not necessary to participate in a course to have experienced this perception or sensation, as it exists in every human being as an authentic aspect of sensory perception '*scopic*' looking drive. During this exercise a kind of relaxed condition is already achieved and is deepened by the parallel exercise of repetition of *Formula-Words* in the thought process. The *Formula-Words* are a pure form of **formal** expressions which are not a part of everyday language or the usual common expression of speech. 'RADICIT' is not a Latin word as one could assume but contains several interlocking meanings in a formulation built as 'linguistic crystal' (an expression that Lacan uses for the structure of the *Unconscious*). Moreover radiat and dicit yield and produce when written in a circle or in

---

used but for confirmation and cognition (for example experiencing the *Pass-Words).*

different alphabetic order several different meanings. For example 'adi cit r' (go on, approach, it moves R) 'C I tradi'(hundred 1 surrender, assign), 'citra di' (the here and now of the gods), ' dicit ra' (so says ra), 'r adic it' (join r add, it goes), 'radi cit (is scratched on, it moves), 'trad ici' (re tell , I have arrived) etc. One can interpret or read several meanings but most of it sounds rather absurd. Yet as formal expression this is of no significance. The decisive factor is only that the statement here is scientifically expounded and clearly demonstrated and this is of utter importance because only then one can fully trust this method and take it seriously.

Once again: sit in a comfortable position, with shut or half open eyes concentrate on *Rays* (Shinning, Phosphorescence, shivering, trickling through) and during this, notionally, purely in thought repeat the *Formula-Word*, or words slowly, monotonously, unhurried and with small interruptions one after the other. This is the first practice or exercise that is actually based or relies on psychoanalysis, because through a mental reverberation a regression is created (an inner retirement) which at the same time concentrates primarily on the narrowed aspects of perception- or scopic- or 'looking drive' (*Id Rays*). It is not sufficient any longer to follow the beliefs and dictates of a meditation teacher or the instructions of a therapist. One has understood that in today's world basic scientific knowledge is available, a known fact that information exists and one has the possibility to think along and with and is not dependent on the ideology of the methods propagated by therapists, teachers which could during the deep moments of an exercise, result in unnecessary moments of irrational angst. The strength of *Rays* (crystalline, mirrored) experience of catharsis is derived from the basic element that exists in all sensory perception, the scopic or 'looking drive'. In fact this is something that is primarily existent in every human being just as the spoken *Speaks* the invocative drive is (linguistic, the announced, the invocation).[15]

Now by the second exercise the attention is drawn to the *Speaks*, which is reported 'It announces"; that is from a level on top of the right side of the head the deep tone, or internal tone arises from the depths of inner self. They are alphabets which the *unconscious* has stored, retained and the internal sounds resound, echo from a 'typographic or topological space'.[9] And exactly in this 'typographic, topological space' the alphabets have infiltrated, rolled in and penetrated the space and have awakened as well as evoked the *Formula- Words*. This is valid here as well:

---

[15] In psychoanalysis we emanate from the finding that in humankind evolution the symbolic order (language) has played an important role dividing perception in sensory acts and in acts of drives. With sensory acts we perceive the reality whereas the drive acts deals with perception-pleasure. In the German language we can distinguish 'Wahr-Nehmung' as 'Truth-Perception' (*Speaks*) and as 'Real-Perception' (*Rays*), so both are in one.

the same procedure occurs that is that the complete primary aspect is relinquished in other words the 'invocative drive" which is a part of every human being, that which is within the *unconscious* adopts the form of brief, compact 'inner sentences', 'ultra-reduced phrases' (definitions which Lacan terms as tone experience) At this primary stage one could be aware only a fine of rustle, a murmuring noise , a distant tone or something similar but the exerciser will experience from the initial stage that here it is to do with concentration based on the top part of the right side or central above of the head related to hearing - speaking system which is related to the 'typographic, topological space' and would fall back upon this.[16]

At a later stage I shall illustrate the point why the second exercise (results) is more of an analytic nature than that of the effect of catharsis. For a relatively long time the two exercises remain separate but after an advanced level the result is that both are connected. Both exercises require about twenty minutes. What is important is that the shift from practical experience and theoretical thought is inter-exchangeable, because only then the end result will be a combination of both: a thought process experience, a logical practice, a cathartic analysis.

---

[16] It does not disturb that by the neurologic aspect the hear-speak-system is situated left-oriented. Firstly there exists a nerve-crossing in the brain and secondly a more rudimental and towards regression leaned right system.

When one has attempted renewed both exercises perhaps one has achieved or gained more experience and I can return to the theoretical aspect once again. In *Analytic Psychocatharsis* formulas are used, which shift on the border of speech (language) and scientifically seen correspond to the concept of psychoanalysis. So one can overcome and lose sight of the remaining differences between meditative methods and psychoanalysis. Hence the actual presence of the teacher at the present moment, the physical presence is finally absent. It is rather due to structures, structural- help, somewhat strong symbolism, word representation, interpretive meanings significantly related (*Speaks*), which nonetheless again at the same time has the parallel structure of crystal clear 'crystalline' (*Rays*). This is precisely the reason why I have considered the actual physical presence of the analyst as disturbing since there is transference between both, the analyst and the person analyzed. A mythical precursor of this condition laden with significant meaning can be traced to the ancient epoch, in antiquity and is none other than the Oracle of Delphi, the impact of which is present even now. In Delphi one could ask a question to the priestess (object of transference) which would be answered in a cryptic sentence (interpretation). So also is the case with teacher and teachings of meditation: the teacher presents a cryptic word, against which one must un-meditate, to able to break away, to be able to move forward and find one's way and finally to be able to find one's own contribution or answer. The same method is known as 'Working out" in psychoanalysis, and fulfills, pertains to the criteria of modern science: whereas the oracle of Delphi or Meditation techniques are constructed and founded on religious mythical-mystical realm of the power of imagination. In *Analytic Psychocatharsis* the words as well or sentences and the Formula Words are naturally not cryptic, but are founded on scientific structures of language even though they could sound cryptic. Here is the fundamental and basic difference.

5. The essence of the Formula-Words

I can no longer leave the reader in the dark regarding the structure and explanation of the *Formula-Words*. The *Formula-Words* corresponds exactly the *unconscious*, what Lacan formulates as that, 'which is structured like a language, like the language of the '*Other*' (the symbolical or the logical). The *unconscious* is through this combination ultimately 'topographic', yes, composed as one could almost say as hieroglyphic (as Image-Word-Sign).[17] It is known especially in dreams as Image-Word-Signs which Freud has referred as the via regia to the *unconscious*. But through a simple slip of the tongue one can also observe this, that three or more image-interpretation could combine to form one word -representation and it happens unconsciously.

To cite an example of the above phenomena there is an anecdote from Heinrich Heine: this is story of a man who wanted to boast about his wealth to Baron Rothschild. The man wanted to say that he was 'familiar' with the Baron, however he said: 'I am so famillionaire with him'. The truth namely is that he was fascinated with the millions, and this simply slipped out from his *unconscious*. And the same way that 'famillionaire' contains multiple

---

[17] The image deals more with the deeper unconscious, the word more with the preconscious. But both could also be mixed.

meanings, namely being familiar and fascinated with the millions (and revelation of his greed), Formula-Words also contain three or more image-like meanings (conceivability / conceptions) as I have demonstrated by the use of the word 'Radicit'. The method of *Analytic Psychocatharsis* is using the *Formula-Words* reciprocal to the slip of the tongue in the above mentioned example namely; it is active and constructive. Though the *Formula-Word* only composes a formulation there are multiple meanings contained in such a formulation or hidden within the flow of words which is awakening and arousing the *unconscious*. As already illustrated, the course of words have multiple interfaces and in this word- flow if one respectively reads or speaks out from one interfacing point to another one arrives at several meanings or different interpretations. It behaves in the same manner as the above mentioned example: one can hear the familiarity, millionaire, or even 'familiar with the millions".

fa mil i l   are

   mil l i on are

fa mil l i on are

Pict. 2: Multiple layers of three meaning corresponding to intonation- illustrative structure and written underneath each other.

Just as multiple word and image representation functions in the *unconscious* so does the *Formula-Words*. This combination of word image representation interfacing one another is similar to the modern technique of computer science. Here it is possible to replace one form of interfacing point to another between two or more systems. If one practices such a repetition in thought - now as already mentioned as constructive, scientific, psycho linguistically constructed - *Formula-Words*, then one has an access to the already given interfacing point composed in the *unconscious* (image/ word, *Rays* / Speaks). So this can be opened and modulated. The *Formula-Words* are so to say small machines, catalytic, accurate pass words that one can send to the *unconscious*. There the psycho linguistic key fits in to the corresponding lock. Such a *Formula-Word*, which henceforth combines clearly image and word representative elements and which in turn originate from Latin that is well suited too, as cited in the example below:

VE-RO-RA-TE

The image representative characteristic of this formulation is in fact as in the case of RADICIT not so well coind but is better displayed in the circular diagram below. Anyhow the alphabets and syllables in this somewhat stylized written manner is certainly something that is image representative. A person with knowledge of Latin would recognize that there are clear words hidden in this. Also the definition of 'linguistic crystal' fits in here rather well. Yet on the other hand not to be too caught up in the theoretical aspect at this stage I would like to mention briefly that the image representative contains aspects of Latin formulations with its precise scientific background, which shall be elaborated later on. What is concealed in the Latin formulation VE-RO-RA-TE, for example: vero rate (through truth it is sure), V ero rate(as five I shall be valid), r at evero (but as r I will be bygone), e ver orat (as E let the spring burn or youth speaks E), rorate ve (do drop? by violence), vero rate(reality through ship or really rat),or at

e ver(burn since youth). Many more meanings lie within (ora means the mouth, faces; orate means also Speak! Pray!) Meanings that are rather nonsensical at the end, quite without any significant importance when read from a different starting point (this is best seen in the circular writing, adjoining picture).

However it is as in a slip of the tongue or as in a dream, which is also often nonsensical but from which psychoanalysis often derives an important hidden sense. This is so since it is not the single and most curious significance which is exercised, but the uniform, composite and clear vocal formulation. Depicting interfaces only serves the purpose of scientific reasoning and linguistic structures. At this point I would suggest that the first exercise from the two mentioned exercises to be practiced once again, founded on the knowledge gained so far. This helps immediately; to begin with the practical experience.

Analytic Psychocatharsis: practical attempt anew

The practical experience should remain in the foreground when it is to do with psychological disorders that express itself in the form of physical ailments. The very fact that it is expressed in the form of physical disorders shows that theoretical considerations and therapeutic attempts to heal the soul has not been always successful or has not sufficiently proved to be of much help. Hence the practical, physical, sensitive- perceptibility side of an ailment must be more emphasised, taken more into consideration.

With the **first exercise** now - as has been already exercised in the previous one and illustrated once again - sit in a relaxed position (with half shut or closed eyes) and note if one can observe something like a SHINE. The formulation that one perceives a 'light' as often underlined and emphasised in meditative methods of relaxation is often unfortunately contradictory. Actually it has little to do with light. The definition *Rays* is far more apt here, as a part of the *unconscious* scopic or looking drive; since most people are able to grasp easily an appearance of brightness, an oscillation. One must concentrate at ease, effortlessly on this and perceive it as a hazy veiled, shivering, drizzling-trickling through. Once this SHINE has been registered within, to a certain extent at least, one must continue without interruption and concentrate, focus and guide one's inner perception towards this direction.

The French Psychoanalyst E. Dolto spoke in this connection, as already referred to as the 'Body Image'. Thereby it deals with something that is raised above one's own individual notion of body image and whose personal perception of Shine is uplifted. There are moments when one can sense, feel and realize this rather than see it. It is to do with the perception that one has of one's own body image based on the inside-outside notion of the self - image that one perceives within the mind's eye; they are the knotted (topographic) organization of the inner image of self. The third diagram illustrates very simply the schema of 'body image' (*Rays*).

(Pict. 3) The illustration in this diagram depicts a very simple, geometrical, topographically reduced figure of a body image (shaded figure). From certain pre-given condition of the psycho-physical center there are accurate, very precise corresponding signals of the body to that of self –image. F. Dolto spoke about basal, dynamic and erotic body image. Here it is only presented as a comprehensive schema, that refers to the *Rays* aspect of body image and could represent more the structural rounded (basal), moving image (dynamic) or phallic figure (erotic). As a total image it could be experienced also as shivering, drizzling, trickling-through as has been mentioned. But it could also be defined as veiled in this case because O the elusive presence of the 'Other' can be sensed behind the half revealed figure.

Does not matter how, but nonetheless what is clear is that someway during this *Rays* one pays attention to the con-generic aspect and simultaneously repeats the so called *Formula –Words* in the mind, in thought. It is sufficient that this *Rays* in whichever way it seems to be or appear has oscillatory characteristics even if it remains black behind closed eyes. It has nothing to do with eyes or with how the word IT *Rays* is prompted. It is only to do with the issue of a passive attention if something, that has anything to do with the character of *Rays* ap-proaches, is perceivable and re-mains. (It is an inner perception of a glowing image that emerges from within, a *Rays* that has per-haps no form, contour, shape, or a particular color but a kind of illu-

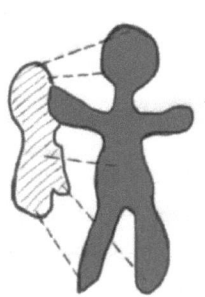

minant presence, a sparkling, shinning vision, a revela-tion that has nothing to do with optic seeing enforced from outer objects. Could be a point or a dot, black or white appearing from the depths of one's being; effortless and easy without any forced attempt). Simultaneously one repeats in thought this or the *Formula-Words* that incorporates the characteristics of an ideal object of meditation. (psychoanalytic term: 'object of transfer-ence').[18] In this phase of practice it is mainly to do with

---

[18] With the *Speaks/Rays* in combination arises that what I like to call an 'translating-object'.

the perception which contains the characteristic of *Rays* and parallel to repeat the *Formula-Words* within the mind which when mutually rocked together intensifies and strengthens.[19]

Once again: after a while, of sitting in a relaxed attentive state of being, a change occurs in every human being, which one could comprehend as cumulative *Rays* catharsis. This is further deepened by the simultaneous repetition of the *Formula-Word*, repeated in thought. This *Rays* or irradiation (gleam / appear), this glimmering something is, as often emphasised a kind of primordial perception and is existent within the *unconscious* in every human being. I suggest now once again that the first exercise is once again practiced but in addition with the new *Formula-Word* (VER- OR –A-TE). It consists, in that, the experience of something that which approaches and has the character of a *Rays* (without the conscious effort

---

[19] The resistance against revealing of the repressed as known in psychoanalysis is sometimes mirroring a resistance against the *Formula-Words*. So one of my students emphasized he had always 'to think on 'radish by the formulation 'Radicit'. By other *Formula-Words* different displacements happened. So I say: all associations are allowed but for exercising *Analytic Psychocatharsis* all – even the Latin-ones - should recede. One is compelled to interpret it from the psychoanalytical stand point if the vocabulary remains on one part of the forehead. That was not difficult for 'radish'. The student associated 'lizzi' and 'eracing'. The latter means in gutter language having intercourse.

of eyesight, without active participation of imaginative thought process). For this purpose the formulation VER-RO-A-TE is simultaneously and now even together (one after the other) with the word 'Radicit', as R.A.D.I.C.I.T.V.E.R.R.A.T.R.A.D.I... . etc. is repeated slowly, monotonously in thought and once again repeated. Through this repetition of the formula it is further sharpened, broadened and imprints itself even deeper in the *unconscious*.

Before I explain the next one again, the second exercise, afresh and deepened, I would like to explain and return to the essence of the *Formula-Words*. Without this the entire procedure would be meaningless, so a clear understanding is essential to proceed further. It is significant that the intellect grasps this as well just as much as the practical experience of the moment is as important. Only then can the intellect during the process of exercise remain undisturbed because then the mind is calm and not preoccupied with anxious, uneasy questions of actual background, or of its roots. Nevertheless - to emphasise beforehand - it has nothing to do with the mystic because here in the *Analytic Psychocatharsis* the intellect is very much present, functional and not absent and one can always refer to it when certain questions emerge. Just as the exercise can always be put into practice so too can the theory be considered, questioned and scrutinized when it is necessary. Such an approach apparently only delays the process of the exercise. Cerebral activity (also termed as 'conjectural") should progress and deepen within this process. Ultimately it is, yes, even a final solution, as accompanied sanction of truth.

Now to return once more to the character of *Formula-Words* and in fact as point of reference one can take the help of the circular diagram. The illustration shows that the *Formula-Words* are written in a circle. Whatever and whichever way one begins is not the focal point but what is essential is to read it in a clockwise manner; a constant mental repetition finally leads one directly to a formulation arising from the *unconscious*. As I have already quoted Lacan, *Id Speaks* in the *unconscious*. Even though *Id Speaks* - in accordance with Freud - with no contradiction, although counterpoints and opposing anticathexis prevails. How could one imagine this? Well, not through a contra speech, but through another kind of speaking within the *unconscious* - an *'other speaking".*[20] One can explain this very well based on the two basic drives which do not contradict one another. Nonetheless they are expressed through a language of the *Other* correlating respectively in what appears to the adverse grounds. And so exactly the *Formula-Words* are constructed: in

---

[20] Briefly and after Lacan: one has to find in the discourse what has the same profound significance in another discourse. The *Speaks* finally has the same profound significance as the *Rays* namely of a basic drive although both are resulting from different discourses. From the linguistic aspect, word-like discourse and from the iconic aspect, image-like discourse.

ORATE VER (Speaks Spring), concealed in VERO RATE as well (I speak the Truth). It has two or more discourses, whose background meanings are quasi squeezed out from the *unconscious* through the exercise of homogenous uniformity of *Formula-Words* (which I term at a later stage, in the second exercise as the performance of *Pass-Word*).

It is clear, that the *Formula-words* thereby must include completely disparate meanings, so that even the most creative thinker cannot find from a conscious concept a collective cluster of meanings, and is compelled to read a direct sense in the meaning. The disparate meanings are as important, as the established fact that they deal with genuine meanings even when it seems illogical or even absurd. One exercises - I emphasise again - not the individual imaginative conceptions, but only the complete, compact, consistent formulations. The analysis in the interface solely serves the scientific cause and the intellectual understanding of the structure of the *Formula-Words*: namely that they are in the same way structured as in the *uncon-*

scious. In the *unconscious* all conceptions together cannot through any kind of conscious construction arrive at a sense. Here once again the image of the circular illustration (Pict: 4).

It functions just like the absurd in dreams (or as the example given earlier 'famillionaire"), that several concepts in the *unconscious* are assembled together but nonetheless contain a significant hidden message. Because - as mentioned earlier - the analyst draws the proper sense out of the so called absurd or nonsensical meanings (hidden within). The teacher of Zen meditation allows his students through the absurdity (nonsense) of 'Koans" to find a sense, to develop and reach a solution or a transformation. Yet similarly, just as important is also the conceptual aspect, that which is conceivable in the 'topological" word-image representation, to create a 'topographic" structure. This knotted or interlocking occurs in the *unconscious*, in the brain, in the hyperspace or whatever one wishes to name it. Diagram 4. Illustrates a Formula-Word that is turned to 180 degree and then the band is pasted together (Mobius band). Just from this point of view it becomes clear that it lets itself turn around in the head, this structure allows itself to pop out as Image-Word anytime. I would at a certain point of time call this Word-Image in analogy to the *Formula-Word*, a *Pass-Word*.

We find support in the intellectual understanding of these *Formula-Words*, which are at the limit of vocalization, because we are living in times in which we have grown accustomed to the intellect and to science, rather than to the primal beliefs of earlier times. Those days we obeyed entities, i.e. defined as God or other manifestations of gods which are no longer applicable in to-days world. In a recent publication of mine, I stressed that the founders of religion probably even used similar meditation as used in the description of the *Formula-Words* here. It is just that they were not explained in a scientific manner, nor were they used in such a manner, thus the explanation was somewhat different. These experiences were explained or seen as divine or manifestation of divinity. However, psycho analysts have not perceived the structure of the *unconscious* in this manner nor have they used it in this pattern. The psychoanalysts have also remained at the point of word association and have not gone beyond or uplifted the possibility of simultaneous pure 'crystal" structure, image representative structure in the *unconscious*. Then no one associates free and deep enough. For the 'physical sick soul" the aspect of image representation 'crystals" are off utmost importance.[21]

Once again: also with *Formula-Words* the image-representative structure of the alphabetic order is as important as the structure of word through it. One can illustrate this image-representative structure even better through another topology as depicted in the diagram 4. But another so called 'endogenic model" which the electronic technicians and doctors in the seventies of the last century have illustrated and now could be seen as a kind

---

[21] Lacan often demonstrated with the help of topological figures like the Moebius-Band or the Boy-Surface how psychic powers are circulating in the brain or in the unconscious realizing *Rays/Speaks* characteristics.

of bridge demonstrating the actual 'subject-image representation" of *Rays* (see Diagram 5), whose meaning is embodied and as well as transmitted through it.

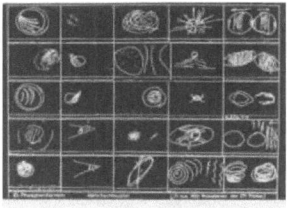

Pict. 5 Down the Topology of Torus, right different models of illustration (from Eichmeier et al. Endogen image models, U&S 1974

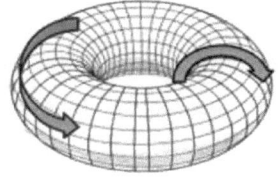

This illustration shows an endogenic model in the form of a luminescence, activated through brain stimulation. This luminescence, on the other hand resembles very much topographical figures, also when they are only simple multiple optical samples. They are obviously in the region between brain and psyche and also through other methods this can be allured here forth. Thereby it shall be indicated that it is not solely dependent on artistic topography. Everything that conveys very well a simple dynamics of optic, be it art, science or mathematic, deals with the same representative form of *Rays*. Yet this is, as such a pure subject oriented experience. Whereas in the dynamic of Torus it can be observed that it strives to a double linear perspective, in the case of endogenic luminescence models the nature is more of small compact, mostly circular images of spontaneity. Torus mirrors in geometrical (topographic) manner the psychodynamic, contrary to image -muster which do it in a luminescing form.

The unconscious in this case -_ by the pure image-representation - is not that challenged to give forth, what I have mentioned above as 'thought experience" respectively termed as *Pass-Word*. For the procedure of *Analytic Psychocatharsis* it appears to me that diagram 4 is most applicable, which I recommend since it demonstrates most clearly the material aspect and as well as combines best the image and word representation. Each person practicing this method certainly will use an individual image-word-representative structure. They would anyway either have a very simple 'topography" or only have a perceptual impression of 'phosphorescence".

And also would develop tight, compact 'inner sentences", hence named, *Pass-Words* (Lacan speaks here now about 'ultra- reduced phrases"). Also art, especially when it is of a very semantic nature, can also be of help and this is the only reason that I have illustrated this diagram. Not otherwise, that I have accentuated art as means of sublimation. *Analytic Psychocatharsis* is nothing else than a uniquely compact, deepened medium towards a comprehension of sublimation.

6. The second exercise and the essence of the Pass-Words

At this stage to the concrete second exercise once again: by this particular exercise the concentration is simply focused on *Id Speaks*. Initially it can sound just like a 'tone' or as Lacan named it: 'a universal murmur'. As already mentioned above, it can operate as 'ultra-reduced phrases', by that all which is within us in the unconscious is articulated and divested, and is directed as such to the '*Other*'. So even the plea or a cry of a child is not just a self-contained expression but is more directed to another, to the '*Other*'. For this reason a child's cry includes a *Speaks*; a call towards someone and is not just simply a snivel or a clangor. The second exercise does not deal with just a cacophony of voices that one hears, also when the definition 'voices' expresses or is closest to this meaning. Exactly through this the tying knot of voices becomes a coherent, unified *Speaks*. This is expressed mostly in the form of a proverb or a poem,[22] than as only just, for example what is termed as 'white noises' in computer science. Nonetheless: these 'white noises" (re-dundancy) is for us of more significance than conscious voices of information! It should bring clarity to the 'un-

---

[22] In their study ‚Brain and Poem' (Schrott, R., Jacobs, A., 2011) the authors have described in extenso such elementary con-nections and knots.

conscious" rather than that which is known. Now once again back to the *Speaks* of 'voices'.

Even Socrates was also dependent - as known - on the voice of his *'daimonion'*, on his 'inner" voice. Thereafter he depended on the voice of simple people and finally yes of his own, his rhetorical philosophical-voice. Even so *Analytic Psychocatharsis* is dependent on the 'voice of Science' (psychoanalysis), second on the voice of *Formula-Words* and lastly on the interpretative voice of *Pass-Words* (possibly under the aid of a therapist). According to Lacan it is to do with 'voice of (psychic) objects'. At another point he speaks also about the accomplishing of the subject under the commandment of the 'voice'; in *Rays / Speaks* the process of psychic stabilization and consolidation. Philosopher Heidegger spoke in this context as the 'chime of silence', which perhaps expresses even better what is meant with *Speaks*. But it sounds somewhat superficially religious.

It does not really matter if one speaks about 'tone', 'murmur' or 'voice'. To avoid any kind of confusion I have brought together all these factors under the definition of *Speaks*. It is only essential to know that as in the case of *Rays,* one must concentrate primarily on that which has the characteristic of *Speaks* in the broadest sense of the term. Initially it does not matter how it sounds. This *Speaks* appears from the top of the right side of the center of the head because it has something to do with speech center in the left area of the brain. One can explain this as echoic repercussions because it resounds as resonance in the right part. But it also has something to do with significant orientation, which in linguistic usage is expressed as an alliance from 'right', 'right', 'rectify' or with the universal chirality (handedness).

Briefly once more: we concentrate now, in the second exercise on something that is within us, that we con-center, i. e. to move together something primordial, archaic from the depth of self. To concentrate on 'The Echo of Discourse' that comes from within. This aspect should become during the exercise to a true and genuine *Speaks*, namely to what I term as *Pass-Word*. They emerge as the echo of innate thoughts arising from the unconscious, and the link with conscious thought is often experienced to a certain extent at least. As is with Freud one can speak about 'unconscious thoughts", that which incorporates *'primal repression'* (I refer to this expression here because it suits a parallel definition of mine, namely 'primal-*transference*").

Now I shall give certain concrete examples for this exercise. Even if one, during this second exercise does not practice directly and simultaneously the *Formula-Words*, the impact of this still naturally remains and governs, hence in the same way these 'linguistic' side (*Speaks*) these so-called 'crystals' (*Rays*). Also this exercise takes about 10 - 20 minutes. For both exercises together one requires approximately about 20 - 40 minutes and the aim of this is that they combine to form one's own distinct personal experience of the *unconscious*. This deliverance occurs through catharsis also an analytic comprehension which is further confirmed and proclaimed by *Pass-Words*.

Psychoanalysis	Analyt. Psychocatharsis	Meditation
"evenly suspended attention"	***Rays***	'light', point
	Formula - Word	
Interpretation of the		suggestions
analyst, free associations		prayers
of the patient	***Speaks***	mantras

Pict. 6 Schema of psychoanalysis, meditation and aspects that has developed *Rays* and *Speaks* as a comprehensive definition for *Analytic Psychocatharsis*

Here, schema 6, demonstrates clearly the similarity and differences of the method experienced. The use of this complex Word-Image representation in *Rays / Speaks* connects with a formula- formulation, as in VE-RO-RA-TE or as in RA-DIC-IT really well, that it is ideal, compact and solid. Yes, one must even say: it is knotted, concentrated, reaches clarity as well. For this reason one can name it when placed face to face as object of *transfer-ence* and the interpretation in traditional psychoanalysis as 'object of translation'. It does not only take over significance, interpretation that conveys a sense but translates also now the mirrored, image -representative part in the word-representation and its objective part in itself is image-representation. When the above mentioned exercise has had an impact, or has conveyed something essential then the result is not just a feeling of relaxation but eventually a kind of Topology.[23] It is an elementary mathematically directly experienced structure that underlies the 'object of translation". Even the earliest form of touch, or various early perceptions have the same pattern namely pure structures, 'topologic" in mental organization, memorized/stored or processed.

Retransmission to the Practice and Character of the *Pass-Words*

Through the repetition of RA-DIC-IT - VE-RO-RA -TE. in thought and simultaneously paying attention to the phenomena of a characteristic of *Rays* one has perhaps reached a relaxed condition and eventually *catharsis* as well. Now (after 10 - 20 minutes) change to the

---

[23] Topology is the teaching of spatiality called Non-Euclidic- or Gum-Geometry. A triangle could have curved lines so that the angular sum could be more or less than 180^0. If the psyche is organized topologically we can imagine it as structured by very flexible but also concrete models or signs.

2.exercise. By the 1.exercise the emphasis in the foreground was to let go, release and relaxation; concentrating on the experience of *Rays* and the repetition of the
Formula-Words. Now in the 2.exercise the concentration
is shifted to the top right side of the head and on *Id
Speaks* (something that is announced), at which stability
and security is achieved. (One has the feeling of sound-
ings, vertical security as though one can fathom a rise or
fall, descend or ascend along the 'announced'. Sometimes thoughts emerge and arise from the wide depths of
the mind, a *Pass-Word* which has a reference as often
noted to the unconscious and makes one aware (self-
awareness).

If one now shifts once more to the 1.exercise this procedure can be further deepened, so that a dialogue takes
place between the repetition of *Formula-Words* and the
emergence of *Pass-Words*. Certainly conscious thoughts
dominate and operate again, rather strongly and one begins to think about the significance of the brief dialogue
before one begins to exercise once again.

The former result is more or less located in the center of
both exercises and emphasised or accentuated on one side
or the other. During the course of the first exercise if the
effect is based more on the spatial kind of objectivity
then the experience of *catharsis* will consist more of
'body image'. It will rest predominantly in the strong
body- image- representation and the experience of *Rays*:

a 'trickling through", a 'shivering release of 'body-image" which will not only bring and enhance a relaxed state of being but will also bring an 'illumination' a light of joy in the form of an inner kind of objective structure. I have spoken earlier on in this context about 'veiled" perception. It is to do with the 'veil" of the '*Other*' .That very O, that Lacan talked about as 'Treasure house of Signifiers", the knots, the navel that hides behind the veil of concealed words.

Psychoanalysis is often a dry issue, contrary to meditative methods, in which reigns an element of ecstasy, frenzy, and even perhaps a bit of intoxication. In *Analytic Psychocatharsis* it will not come so far but an echo of ecstatic intoxication may resound. Then naturally also here (by the emphasis on spatial-object-representation) a minimal 'speaks" is already present, this is why I have written it small letters and also in quotation marks. The result is that more a SHINES/ 'speaks' but has nonetheless something of a basic structure of space, spaciousness as such, hyper -space (interlaced boxes of spatial dimension) I can only refer to Freud here, Freud's idea of spatial-image reference of the unconscious; whereby it is so structured as when the city of Rome is presented as packages of intertwined epochs, all locked together from the antique to middle ages as well as buildings and structures of modern times.

If we find ourselves in the course of the exercises more on the side of *Id Speaks*, then the characteristic of time-interpretation predominates. The character of a kind of time will be in the fore- ground of the exercise and a *'shines" / Speaks*. Now we arrive at the point which Freud named as dream which are 'key-sentences" i. e. pregnant, brief formulations, that have clear meanings and do not require to be vastly interpreted. I have already mentioned Lacan's 'inner-sentences" or 'ultra-reduced" phrases, which are almost adept as complete sentences, audible, and ascertainable in thought. It is as though a brief thought from wide away and from the deepest depths surfaces, almost audible, even truly 'announced" a key that the 'unconscious" presents. Exactly in the same manner as in fact the actual analytic procedure reveals, but here it is more direct, objective and all conclusive (as 'voice of objects"); I name it as the perfect "translation" from the unconscious, an identity word, a *Pass-Word*.

I can depict this experience through a very humorous example: A person who was extremely critical of *Analytic Psychocatharsis*, but who had nonetheless been exercising it for a good while, suddenly thought as if from far away, as if an inspiration, or as if he had actually almost heard it : 'Nothing Said"! Yet at that precise moment, he realized that that something had been said namely two words 'Nothing Said"! But it wasn`t only this experience that convinced him of the functional method of *Analytic Psychocatharsis* but he understood more how the dynamics of the unconscious is constructed, namely, often through anticathexis through an 'other way round of the unconscious. As he was conscio'usly aware, he was of the opinion that this method of psychotherapy was utterly nonsensical, meaningless and 'said nothing'. However his unconscious pushed him at that moment to a revelation, a realization or authentic interpretation that he had had a resistance, that is unconscious actually spoke a 'truth' because it like a word of the *'Other'*, the *'Other'* that is within us and all compassing as well. And even though it dawned upon him that this was something of his own, within him, he still had the feeling as though it were someone else, a teacher, or an interpreter who had placed this in him. The characteristics of anticathexis is exactly what Freud named as *primal repression*, something, that traditional method of psychoanalysis does not draw near too and whose parallelism to *primal transference* I have already explicitly proven in *Analytic Psychocatharsis*.

Another further example of this: this is of a person who had been practicing the method of *Analytic Psychocatharsis* for a certain period of time. He was very interested in questions dealing with religious content, even though he did not belong to in any particular religious denomination or faith. During the course of practicing this method for almost about half an hour he was about to end it, when his thoughts surfaced from the depths and were almost audible (according to his own depiction): 'Let us steal the fourth book!" For him as well as for me -

as I was aware of his religious interest - it was pretty clear, relatively fast that, that it must have something to do with a Book of Faith. In all probability this had to do with books of monotheism which the Old as well as the New Testament and the Koran practices. It is so a -typical of the unconscious that it does not emphasise 'Let us write the fourth Book!' This would be the typical wish of a dedicated Orthodox, gripped and over- whelmed by pious Orthodox devotion. Because for somebody like this the three Books of Faith are not sufficient enough. No, here in the case of my test person speaks the *unconscious* with its characteristic anticathexis, almost *Oracle* like prophecy. The fourth alphabet does not exist and neither can one write it. One can only actually steal it! And one can steal it only within oneself.

Then the impact is like stealing when one shifts it from the depths of the self and allows it to ascend. One can only in this instance steal it from the self. Well then, ob- viously it is again meant as the relevant self here. Then such a religiously interested person must allow himself to be of course indoctrinated that which all the Religious Books do not really fulfill, or provide answers too to his quest. They can stimulate and inspire one to be occupied with questions of religion. But they will not lead to, where those have been guided who had written these books (or lead one in whose Name they were written) I have expressed this elsewhere; over the almost extinct ability or capacity towards Revelation.[24] My test person has turned now to *Analytic Psychocatharsis* because of this, even though he has searched further and long, including and adding books; as well as catechisms, sermons on religious contexts and spiritual, psychic, mental matters or what-ever one chooses to name it. And thank god he has found and arrived to the information: to come closer to the sacred /sacral one must commit a sacrilege, one must steal from one-self; this theft is from within. (*ek me auton,* as Heraklit once said, from me here forth).

You can - so a further interpretation - reach and find the Truth on the path already followed by the philosophers earlier on, by treading on the same footsteps so to say, namely through thesis and anti- thesis: through a certain element of paradox. The *unconscious* does not say (and also God manifested would not say today), 'read the great Books of Faith!' No, you must put aside your ego, your conscious self, your ego-ideal, and ideal ego, your omniscience and your belief at religious denomination. Only It or perhaps (one is allowed to say He or any other name) reveals the Truth. Steal from all the pseudo–scientific and mythical utterances that circulate all around the world. The truth lies within yourself and you have to find it there and only there will you find it. And you have to do it yourself, stealing is a hard task. It is analysis as well as *catharsis.* 'Let us steal the fourth Book", this has

---

[24] Hummel, v., G., Signifier God, BoD (2013)

a liberating effect, a *catharsis*, for the relevant person concerned as well.

I emphasise once again: it is something quite different, when the practicing user in the first example was critical of the method, doubtful with himself, and had misgivings for a time about his conscious thoughts: but yet, yes, perhaps there is something in the method after all. There is 'something said". The second example of the practicing user is that one day he arrived at the point and conviction: I should write something further about religion. Both were through outward logic only partly convinced. But all this as it surfaced from the inner depths, as if something strange from within his innermost self, yes precisely as the 'voice of the Object', which is the main objective here, approached from within then the conviction was of a different kind.

Suddenly as though it surfaced, the 'universal murmur" found a voice, (the tones, chimes, rings, whisper, murmur and announcement etc.) exactly those *'Otherness'* in the unconscious that have egressed audibly, stepped out from the inner shell. Suddenly the tones and the 'universal murmuring" from within brought forth just such a differentiation. The *Other* itself (inside and outside) has spoken.[25] It has called out from within the veiled self. First

---

[25] In Lacans psychoanalysis the *Other* is an important idea. He says that the unconscious is the language of the entire *Other*

and foremost this creates mainly 'a key like experience' an awareness (analytic) and in addition something of *Psychacatharsis* (liberating and cleansing). In the process of such an experience like the: 'Nothing said!' or the 'Stealing of the fourth book!" and the subsequent elucidatory insight into the meaning, has actually nothing to do with the mystic. It is the unconscious that appears and is heard here as an 'ultra –reduced' phrase (*Speaks*) and also *Rays* since the 'nothing said" is such a brief, almost image-like formulation or momentary lightning, that also produces a light cathartic feeling.

The 'Voice of Object' has something to do with the Subject-Being. Only when the psychic 'Object" finds a voice - even if this is present in a metaphorical sense - will real justice be done to a human being in its status as a subject. The 'free association" provides naturally also a voice but it is the voice of a neurotic, yes a voice of one's neurosis, to a 'rigmarole" talk prompted ego. In contrast, though the voice of *Pass-Word* exists as more distant-ego yet it is nonetheless a clear, direct voice of the subject insinuated to the unconscious. This voice cannot be defined as the 'objective' voice as is known in the traditional sense of natural -sciences. But it is even more so, an 'objectified" voice. It is a voice that can at last

---

resounding within ourselves. Briefly, it is the *Rays/Speaks* in us.

satisfy the thousand year old dispute between philosophers over the issue of man as a Subject or an Object.

The fact that these 'inner-sentences', these *Pass-Words* are so precise, and are so briefly 'ultra-reduced", that they have the same function as the *Formula-Words* in their brevity and precision. The *unconscious* is stimulated through such compact, multilayered formulations (incidentally, 'nothing said' or in the sense that one 'must steal') just as are the *Formula-Words* animated through this brevity of precision. As I have already mentioned, that these chronologically brief scanned, translated-transferred *Pass-Words* tilt and belong more towards *Speaks*; *catharsis* with its expansive spatial liberation tilts more towards *Rays*. Certainly most of the results - as illustrated in the given examples – are a combination of both. *Formula*–and *Pass-Words* both have their own category or effect of multifaceted meaning/significance (more than three are necessary for the unconscious, so that it can begin to move, circulate, and open up) to a personal formulation.

The ideal combination is when the *Pass-Words* and *catharsis* occur simultaneously, one can be then sure that the *Pass-Words* are applicable. Then in the state of cathartic switching, the behavioral pattern is like switching on and off, off before one sleeps and on when awakens, as is relevantly experienced in analytic interpretation. Here confirms an affective highlight the relevant truth, the 'objective', and the other way round the relevant truth effects a highlight (as the awake-sleep–switch dependably functions). One should not be afraid that one's ego/self is lost when the *Pass-Word* sounds a little strange. Also when the coincidence of *catharsis* and *Pass-Word* is not fully functionally synchronized, the Pass-Word then - as demonstrated - can be explained through analytic reflection and question. In the case of an extreme case a therapeutic consultation can be of importance.

I think that now, it is sufficiently clear how *Analytic Psychocatharsis* functions, that basically seen it is simple and yet precisely scientifically accurate. The exercises begin with a simple specified primary processed reduced *Rays* and *Speaks*, in doing so both elementary conditions are held together through a 'linguistic crystal" of *Formula-Words*. The final effect of the exercises brings in addition a richer, 'higher", complex result, as well as in the sphere of catharsis as well as in analytic field, hence generating a perfect 'translation" (that the process in the unconscious perfectly translates). A certain element of intellectual inquiry for a period of time or once in a while is necessary. Through which this method can be better understood, but also for practicing the exercises a special clarity and feeling of security can be reached.

This procedure not only gives a formal analog but also a real answer from the unconscious. The constant repetition of formula- representative formulations guides one back to the demands of intrinsic energy of the drives and exactly this effectuates also the interpretation of the psychoanalyst. It was also Freud's vision to build a science for everyman. He expressed this wish in an article 'Layman's analysis". So, also now a science for the lay man; so that even a layman can understand *Analytic Psychocatharsis.* For instance one could, e. g. find better Formula-Words or carve out factors that makes the experience of *Rays* somewhat simpler, lighter while it is not always naturally so easy to succeed easily - how I propose here - simply to make an attempt from this brochure. It is the same for *Speaks*. Some person understand straight away a sentence, perhaps because they 'listen" or even better: experience directly. Others in contrast do not understand this significance completely but (feel) sense it, that something has been said that is of importance. In this case one can draw on psychoanalytic appendage which is abundantly available, especially in Lacan and utilize them for oneself or for structuring this method.

7. Simplified summary and a further *Formula-Word*

Simply formulated, *Analytic Psychocatharsis* is nothing else than a deviation of channelized thought process, that is more relevant than those what I have just now formulated as 'everyday" language. We suffer due to a trivial, externalized life style. Many of the psychosomatic symptoms can be explained or diagnosed as a form of unfulfilled mode of life and living. But this is not a method, that compels us, to occupy oneself with the self, on the other hand assigns us to differentiate, to multilayered, thoughtful and sometime to an aspiring level of standard, is this not an ideal method? A method, not only to rid of symptoms and reach an understanding, but also to release oneself from general triviality. This method must not only be practiced but must be grasped and understood in theory as well and that means that perhaps also a general knowledge over the connecting areas should or could be read. (A certain erudite knowledge is required.) Certain psychoanalytic literature could be of help, but also general information on to-days science may suffice.

Human beings are strongly stamped with order that have little to do with a S but with meaning/ significance, symbols and words. In psychoanalysis, one moves therefore from that which is virtually known as *speaking drive*[26] that articulates constantly within us and stands vis-à-vis 'scopic" or looking – drive. Usually the psychic tends to builds a strong defence-mechanism against the impact of power- drives: suppression, somatisation or even differentiation in deep spiritual content. In psychoanalysis one tries to resolve the defences, whereas in the exercises of *Analytic Psychocatharsis* to a large extent, one tries to tangent the defences or tries to dissolve it in another way. [27] Whereas in the method of psychoanalysis, the therapist self becomes the Object of transference of different meaning and interpretation of the mental life of the patient itself , in *Analytic Psychocatharsis* there is no such Object. Instead the exercising user here receives a kind of 'objective" **Key** (Key -sentence that can even incorporate and contain parts of interpretations) that the user can hold on to, that can even assist him from the point of view of pure formulation (subject/ object reference) to achieve certain order in the power-drives, what is attempted in psychoanalysis through long hours of conversations and takes a considerably, long and complicated amount of time.

---

[26] Lacan speaks of the invocation drive.

[27] By the experience of catharsis some of the defense-mechanism are solved because the unconscious drive behind this could find a new destination in the experience of catharsis in combination with *Pass- Words*

The key cannot only originate from the category of B e i n g, it must - as mentioned above – consists by a significant knot itself. The meaning/significance of these knots should not have pre given notions and for programmed interpretations but the unconscious must within the self be able to decipher or decode at its will. It does not necessarily have to be a complete sentence. Just an expression, a word, which is not even a part of language, suffices. In its hidden depth, seen from the pure structural concealed content has a significance and a meaning. Linguists have meant that a sentence, to cite an example _ "colourless green ideas sleep furiously" though from the point of grammar is correct but is quite meaningless. But everyone knows that 'green ideas" (politically viewed) can also be 'colourless" and could be 'frightfully sleepy" (because it is concealed in a drawer) He knows that also with this, that in this context no sentence is meaningless. The sentence of the linguist is just too little codified.

Contrary to this, as seen in RA-DIC-IT and VE-RO-RA-TE we already have in the first part such a key. These Latin words with its quantitative expression carries several meanings, though none can predominate the other (see the main text) If one exercises the key-sentence purely in thought as in meditation, then the unconscious will unlock and release its meaning, especially because RA-DID-IT or VE-RO-RA-TE have multiple meanings and because of this has not one single specific significance. When one practises this as in meditation: this can only be found by each individual subject , as the empirical self, that this particular sentence - as often described in the main part of the text (i.e. page 20). This meaning can be found and discovered, when one practises this as in meditation by each individual subject, by the empirical self that this specific sentence as often emphasised in the main part of the text (i.e. page 20) is of significance. Finally towards the end he would receive as a part of the second key in the form of one or many PASS-WORDS.

For practising the method of *Analytic Psychocatharsis* one requires mostly several *Formula-Words*. Two are too less. At least three or four are necessary. This is the reason why I am illustrating a further *Formula-Word*. One begins in thought after repetition of the *Formula-Words* one after the other and closes this and begins once again after three or four of them.

After R_A_D_I_C_T_V_E_R_O_R_T_E_ one can now include O_R_S_A_C_E_R_A_M as well, in which the following meaning is disclosed: C eram orsa (I shall begin hundred times), amo R sacer (I love the holy R) cera morsa(the bitten wax), mors acer (death is bitter), amor sacer (love is holy) etc. As already emphasised , one can immediately forget these meanings. What is really of importance is that one grasps how the *Formula-Words* are built up, so that one is always ready to see behind this from the stand of scientific-intellectual thought. That is any time one wishes to do so. If any feel-

ings or angst /fear crops up during this procedure, thoughts that
are not welcomed one can con-
template or one can inform oneself further on this particular
method or one can continue to
practice. Blind faith is not wanted or palatable.

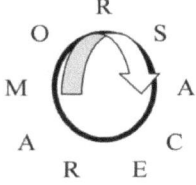

The best and ideal way is to have perhaps four to five
Formula-Words, that one can practice one after the other.
More than five would a bit too much, because it will not
be really possible to retain so many at one go. Three or
more are essential, that one has a continuation, but at the
same time one has to see that one does not become weary
of the same representation of monotonous word-tone. I
wish to emphasise once again that despite the apparently
meaninglessness of the significance of the *Formula-Words*, nonetheless to note, that the interfacing-knots
(inter-lacings) are of great importance and as such cannot
be taken as generated by accident or produced through
computer technique.

So to say they are not impulsively fabricated. The psychoanalytic foundation guarantees one of the security and
seriousness of the method whereas a machine despite its
formal perfection would appear to be rather mechanical,
soulless and hollow . As appendage I wish to include that
Analytic Psychocatharsis can be practised alone, through

instructions given in the brochures or eventually also from the main text. One does not require an institution or academic facilities to be able to practise this method. One can of course inform oneself so from me or from those who have mature experience of this and have practised this method for a while.

Recommendations for further study of literature

Freud, S., Abstract of Psychoanalysis, Fischer TB (1996).

Hummel, v. G., Analytic Psychocatharsis, BoD (2011)

Lacan, J., The Four Basic Concepts of Psychoanalysis, Walter-Verlag (1980).

Website of the Author: analytic-psychocatharsis.com
where one can also find several articles in English about psychoanalysis and the method of *Analytical Psychocatharsis*.

Additional publications of the author

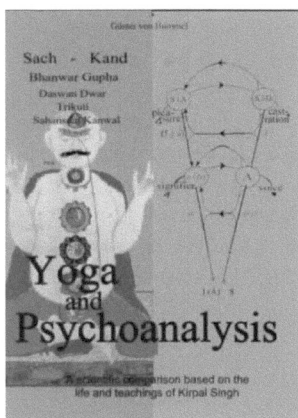

Yoga and Psychoanalysis - This book offers a brief overview of the different types of Yoga and provides a comparison with the modern science of J. Lacans psychoanalysis. Laya-Yoga, as it was taught by the Kirpal Sing (1894-1974), is widely known in India. This study of western and eastern 'spiritual ways" centers around so-called Formula-Words which are quite similar to mantras. The comparative study culminates in an independent and new method which can connect Yoga and psychoanalysis in an ideal way.

What about the ONE
The One is only insufficiently described in mathematics. It is about the spiritual-physical unity of man, which can only be achieved through a combination of psychoanalytical and meditative exercises. The author describes this process using the literature of Siri Hustvedt and other female authors as well as the psychoanalysis of J. Lacan.

A Path to self-analytical Practice

The vertical Ego

Our usual social Ego is oriented horizontally, but the essential and still predominantly unconscious Ego is oriented in the vertical. This is connected with primary inner psychic reflections, which are not exactly captured by psychoanalysis, because it is more oriented to the word. With a few meditative exercises one can reach the sufficiently good vertical and unite it with the horizontal.

Günter von Hummel

Outsmarting Death Two Times

Life while Dying, a treatise on Sisyphus and on a new Self-practice for today

Outsmarting Death two Times.

Neuroscientists have found that after medically determined death there is still a short span (minutes to hours) of brain activity. This phase correlates to a psychically strongly regressive state, which can be grasped beyond psychoanalytic understanding with the procedure of Analytical Psychocatharsis. It is a life while dying that one can still learn before and also experience positively before the absolute end.